ABSOLUTE ZERO

POEMS BY DAVID LUNDE

ABSOLUTE ZERO

POEMS BY DAVID LUNDE

Mayapple Press 2018

Published by   Mayapple Press
                362 Chestnut Hill Road
                Woodstock, NY 12498
                mayapplepress.com

ISBN 978-1-936419-80-7
Library of Congress Control Number

ACKNOWLEDGEMENTS

The author would like to thank the editors of the following publications
in which many of these poems first saw print:

*Aboriginal Science Fiction, Asimov's SF Magazine, Beloit Poetry Journal, Buffalo
Arts Review, Cthulhu Calls, Dark Alley, Dreams and Nightmares, Escarpments, Fig-
ment, Gateways* (A Festshrift for Frederik Pohl edited by his wife, Eliza-
beth Ann Hull), *Howling Dog, Jam
To-Day, Magazine of Speculative Poetry, Midnight Zoo, Mother Earth News,
Pandora, Poetry Northwest, Poetry Now, Poets of the Fantastic Anthology, Raw
Nervz, Rocket Candy Anthology, SFPA Broadside, SFWA Bulletin, Song, Star*Line,
Strange Horizons, Terra Incognita, The Count Dracula Fan Club, The Ghazal Page,
The Silver Web, The Vampire's Crypt, Triquarterly, Turbocharged Fortune Cookie,
Turbocookie, Uncommonplaces Anthology, Wind, Wordsmith*

Book and cover design by Judith Kerman; Hubble Image Credit: NASA,
ESA, J. Trauger (Jet Propulson Laboratory) used under Creative
Commons; Photo of author by Patricia McKillip. Book designed with
titles in Hypatia Sans Pro and text in Californian FB.

Contents

Absolute Zero

Some nights I think that the stars
have died

Already died and these bright photons
left over

Just waves of luminous spaghetti seen
end on

Millions of years from now will abruptly
just stop

But I will never know being already
dead too

Before all the old light is used up
and you

Whoever you are that remain planted
on Earth

Will watch the last red-Dopplered quanta
so weary

With distance weighted with despair
too tired

Even any longer to be but their message
is clear

At last and you are the ones the
only ones

Who will ever truly understand this
and believe

That all any person, plant, microbe, fire,
or rock

Has ever done was to busy itself
with dying

And by now the ambient temperature
of space

Having held steady at 3 degrees Kelvin
almost forever

Begins to fall toward the black hole
of zero

And what will you think as you feel
yourself go

Wherever all of everything and the light and dark
have gone

Tycho

(Tycho Brahe, 1546-1601)

Tycho tended to lose his head,
and that cost him his nose, not quite
the dueling scar of preference,
but Tycho, not one to fret
over the worthless opinions of others,
put on a bold new face
with a nose crafted of silver and gold.
I think he must have had that kind
of total self-belief that captures
cultists, with a P.T. Barnum twist.
He so impressed the King of Denmark
(in spite of—perhaps because of—
the full-grown elk which never
left his side) that he funded,
just for him, Europe's best observatory.
Tycho used it well to disprove Pythagoras,
Plato, and lickspittle Aristotle
who said that all beyond the moon
was changeless, eternal, and so
could not explain the nova Tycho saw,
nor the comet six years later
which broke the crystal spheres
and freed the stars forever.

Imagine him at Prince Rudolph's table,
feeding tender turnips to his elk,
his dwarf Jepp scuttling
after scraps beneath the board,
and meanwhile pumping Kepler
for his math, while Johannes,
in his turn, cajoled from Tycho
data to back his Laws...
or think of Tycho's changeless grief
for the elk that broke its leg
on the palace stairs and died,
think of Tycho taking off his nose
and falling into bed to weep
beneath his new-found stars each night.

Dear Schrodinger

Regarding your comment,
"I don't like it, and I'm sorry
I ever had anything to do with it,"
...quantum mechanics, that is,
well, gosh, we're all sorry
about it, but there it is: virtual
particles keep effervescing out of &
back into the quantum foam (read
nothingness) unless some random
energy pulse empowers them
with reality; particles that once
were intimate with each other
still act out their marriage after
separation, however distant;
their positions are statistical
abstractions, never being more
that 50% probable & even at
36 nanokelvins they refuse to
be less than a skidmark; electrons
go on leaping from one orbit to another
without crossing the space between;
so you might as well stop
bitching and buy cat food.

Plate Tectonics

The continent sinks
earth wrenches open
hell yawns at his feet
magma rises
from its own ashes
the magnetic poles
switch places
a choleric wind
occludes the vision
dawn withers
in the tumbling mountains
ice begins
its aggression
the poet
begins his ode
to structural deformation.

Song of the Martian Cricket

I shouldn't come out here
so many nights, turning
my faceplate to the black sky
with the tasteless, artificial air
whispering in and out of my lungs—
the only sound besides the directional beep
from Marsbase below, a subaudial promise
of security, but not comfort.
It's not the pressure suit I mind
so much, not even the bottomless
black bucket of stars—I miss the moon
pregnant with promise, and the light,
grassy breeze coasting over the hill
to blow the soft strands of your hair
across my lips, and the sound of crickets
grinding their legs with need. Still,
I come out too often and stare
into the abyss of years, then rise,
feeling almost bodiless in the low gravity,
and drift back to the floodlit dome
small and forlorn beneath
its protective covering of dust.

Singularity Song

Sometimes I imagine I can hear it,
That sub-subsonic thrum, a B-flat
57 octaves below middle C,

orders of magnitude below the threshold
of even an ocean-spanning
sperm whale's song,

a bass below bass audible only
by inference, the cosmic drone note,
last vibratory groan of swallowed

stars, a ripping of atomic bonds
on such a scale it makes your
bones ache light years distant.

I do not think it is merely noise,
not just the seeming signal
of a pulsar's regular static strobe,

but a ululating throat-song
that singularities willy-nilly
sing each other, a call

that signals all the other singular
deep-voiced singers that still
another galaxy has fallen in

upon itself, and the space
it once defined now contracts
to zero, drawing with it

the formerly receding fundamental units
like a balloon deflating, and then,
when the holes have swallowed

all the all there is,
they foreshorten space with warps,
drawing together into a point

so small it's just
here(t)here gone,
a metaparticle leaping

to a higher state, and then,
in a single heave disgorging
the ripened energetic seed

of a spanking new universe
with a metacosmic squall
that someday will inform

other hapless lifeforms that once,
at a quantifiable time and distance,
they were born and doomed to die.

Dark & Light

It's night of course;
it always is, isn't it? Universal,
and I speak literally. Dark
is the natural state of things—
dark matter, dark energy, making up
ninety-six percent of the universe
we think of as our own

& the light
we survive by and worship
nothing but a trivial aberration,
despite the dependency of such entities as us.

Yes, let there be Light! Ah, the Glory!
that brings forth life upon the sludgy stones
kludging lonely in the dark...

each luminous object expelling its substance
into the dark, quantum by quantum—
light the visual manifestation of decay,
like corpse-light, a celebratory sort of sparkle
surrounding indomitable entropy.

Port City Lament

No man can go where the deep ships go.
We curse our human flesh that bars the way
and stare at stars that we can never know,

stars as bitter-bright as methane snow.
Our cyborg Pilots bring us tapes to play—
no man can go where the deepships go.

In Port City taverns the holos glow
with vibrant worlds that make old Earth seem gray.
We stare at stars that we can never know,

at worlds on which our vat-spawned children grow,
while robot mothers tend them at their play.
No man can go where the deepships go,

but only load, repair, refuel, and tow,
and wipe his hands and speed them on their way.
We stare at stars that we can never know.

We curse the bread, we curse the dough,
we curse the God that made us from such hapless clay.
No man can go where the deepships go:
we stare at stars that we can never know.

The Singularity in Cygnus X1
Viewed with Pity for HDE 226868

Poor Hildegarde
her white, white arms
her hair
streaming
like Ophelia's
in the black current
helpless
in the unnatural grip
of the vampire
the dancer in the dark
who whirls her
giddy with desire...

NB: The black hole in Cygnus was identified by the matter being sucked
into it from a nearby star. I have taken the liberty of renaming HDE
226868 "Hildegarde".

Message from the Stars

We who are dead now greet you! We who inhabit the cities of dust. We welcome a new mind to the universe. We say, "Child, here is my knee. Here was my knee." This dust, these molecules, these atoms, these quarks. This collection of quarks says, "Hello!"

It's a brand new cosmos. For you. We are already dead. But we greet you. We have a message: you are not alone. We were here. Do not fear.

For you we heat this hydrogen. Do you see it? Do you hear it? Do you feel it? Do

your sensory orifices detect this sign? Do you register by whatever means these radiant pulses? Does your hide twitch? Do your cilia bristle? We attempt an anomaly, a signal to stir all senses. We think there must be commonalities among all beings: responses to radiation, hunger, the urge to procreate, and for intelligent beings, curiosity. We wish you to know we were here!

But no, it is not megalomania, this urge to wrap the cosmos in our self.

It is loneliness. Ah, child, late born child, whose face we will never smell, whose eyes we will never touch...

Hello! Hello and farewell.

Apostrophe to Stars

Stars, I have walked among you
in lands where the first men walked
after the fire subsided
into its veil of ashes.
My father named your names:
Betelgeuse, Aldebaran, Polaris—
friends from his youth
sailing the dark seas, fellow
voyagers in the mystery
which surrounds us. So near
you seemed then, suspended
at arm's length above
the red desert, touching
the horizons of Earth
with curious fingers of light.
Unwearied by distance or time,
which for you does not pass,
frozen in small crystals
of quanta, you fall even now
on my wondering eyes
with messages that say, "Cousin,
we are here, where are you?"

The Spider's Dream

is of an endless dark
beset with luring lights,

of filaments that reach
into each forgotten niche

among the bric-a-brac
of worlds and stars

and loop galactic globes
and spirals, shrouding each

in delicate, dustless lace,
invisible nets of monosilk

that wait to snare unwary
photophilic souls

beating haplessly toward light
in the aching, hungry dark.

The Pioneer Anomaly

With the Kuiper Belt behind them,
Sol's last frontier outpost,
theory suggests they should be speeding up,
the two Pioneer spacecraft, accelerating
just a little, as the sun's gravitational tentacles
begin to loosen, but instead they're slowing,
just slightly, while baffled scientists scrabble
for answers: Dark Matter? Dark Energy?
Thermal radiation from the craft itself?
But all are insufficient to explain
more than 30% of the retardation,
and I think it is merely reluctance,
like schoolchildren dragging their feet
as the big yellow bus pulls up to the curb
for the first time ever.

Of Stars

The Milky Way swirls, a wizard's cloak of stars;
around we wheel on a slim spoke of stars.

Honor that most clever, most sapient ancestor—
when first he spoke, he spoke of stars.

Babylonians connected the dots: Capricorn, Cancer & Leo,
Scorpio, Aries, Pisces, & Taurus with a yoke of stars.

Earthbound too long, we chafe in gravity's chains;
but our planet, too, bears the folk of stars!

Stories tell of alien beings more advanced by far,
even that we are nothing but the joke of stars.

What prospects has the stellar prospector,
eyes blind with glory, poke full of stars?

What will you think at the end, silly maker of poems,
still unknown, unread, ailing and broke—of stars?

For Apollo 16

The crescent moon   and just over it
a star   like the Turkish flag
and Sharon says   when the moon lies
on its side   it is full of water
Then Venus   above it   is dipping her toes
with a shivery grin   and below it
the Stockton antique barn   is sinking
into the creek   but we do not see it
because it rained all afternoon   the first
spring rain   and then
the sun came out   and now
mist thickens   and obscures Stockton Sales
and we can see nothing   below the brimming moon
Oh   it is a nice conceit   but we don't buy it

If there were water   and not rock
or rock   that cupped water
if there were blood in the stone
to be squeezed   but there is not
there are only   the few gallons of men
to stand in a pool   quietly   reflecting
the earth   like a clock in an empty room

Pilot, Pilot

Your eyes were mirrors then,
silver as pressure domes, your
head raked back fifteen degrees.
The angle of your long neck
against the unwholesome horizontal
of that Port City street, the taut
cords of muscle straining
in my sweat-slick fingers,
are a senso I can't erase—
neither that image nor the shame,
knowing even then it wasn't you
I hated, brother, but myself, my life—
and at my back, suddenly, the laughter,
hurrying near, the great laughter,
and you beginning to, your lips
beginning to crimp at the edges
just a bit as if to smile—you!
smile!—and I stared hard
at your eyes—at, not into—
trying to scan His approach
and afraid, so afraid to turn,
as if by not seeing straight-on
I would not be seen. But I was.

That fearsome hand, irresistible
and deft as a waldo, slipped loose
my grip, set us apart by a meter,
you cursing weakly, rubbing your throat
where my thumbs had bruised it,,
both of us weeping like children
caught in some infantile squabble,
pulled casually apart and forgotten,
while He cruised unruffled off,
murmuring, "Easy, grounders, easy there."
Oh, easy, always easy for Him!
cruising off to His future,
off to His ships and His stars.

"But we made you!" I screamed,
and the fury was in me then, so huge
I flicked out blade and flung it
hard at His enormous back—
and how He did what He did then
I can't tell you; I couldn't see
but whirling flash and blur and hear
the shree-kaslam of its return.
Then He was gone. My blade
was buried to its hilt in a wall
of solid ferrocrete. The empty street
still echoed with His laughter.

I am not Arthur Pendragon
and have no hope. I suppose
I could have left Port City,
walked off those bitter streets,
but where is there to go
that matters? I can't forget
the mirrors of your eyes,
how they could not frame
His fearful symmetry, how they
diminished and diminish me.

Moonwalk

Look at them:
        afraid
of the ground,
my feet
        fat and far away
  trip, trap
on the nerveless regolith.

No goatfoot, I:
only my footprints
singularly remember
        me here.
  tock, tock
the lead clock
of decay
pipes in the rock
of entropy
to stay my stay.

Extragalactic Voyage

So there were no stars
there where the Old Ones went,

so there was no fire
before the Old Ones' tent,

so there was no water
in the sea where they'd been sent,

so there was no earth
to take back what was lent,

so dust incorruptible
was what that finally meant,

and we can only wonder,
wonder at their intent.

A Picture Postcard of the Cerne Abbas Giant

      The giant faces the sky, his left hand open in welcome, his right clenched
firmly to the haft of a knotted club. His rampant and prodigious penis must also
be a threat or promise.
      The giant reclines stiffly on a sloping Dorset hillside. From both air and
ground his outline carved into the white limestone is bold against the green of spring
grass.
      How many centuries has his triple gesture made its wordless guarantee?
Whose eyes is it intended for? Surely not for men alone, the men there dwarfed
beneath his feet.
      Lords of the sky, I am ready, he says.
      Here is the open hand.
      Here is the club of war.
      Here is the organ of love.
      I am ready, Lords.

Cosmonauts Give Russia Space Lead

[Voskhod 1, 12 October 1964]

Three Soviet Spacemen hurtled
around the globe on a flight
that leapfrogged the Russians
into the lead in the space race.
"Attention, attention! The crew
from the spaceship *Voskhod*
is sending best wishes, peace
and happiness to the American people."

James E. Webb, Administrator, NASA,
said the Soviet accomplishment was
"...a clear indication that the Russians
are continuing a large space program
for the achievement of national power
and prestige."
            The man on the street
in Moscow seemed to take the news
casually as it came over loudspeakers
on a gray, chilly morning. But a crowd
gathered in Red Square and tossed
military men jubilantly into the air.

[a found poem]

Einstein's Cold Equation Blues

It used to be so easy
blasting into space:
my home-built backyard rocket
would take me anyplace.

The Stars My Destination,
Non-Stop off I'd go,
until I made *First Contact*
out in Scorpio.

At the thunder of my landing,
Who Goes There? you would say,
(*All You Zombies* wondering
how you got that way!).

I'd *Skylark* off to Vega,
cruising at *Tau Zero*,
and outsmart bug-eyed monsters,
a *More Than Human* hero.

Out Around far *Rigel*
on a lazy day I'd roam,
'til I finally lensed your message
through stars like drifting foam:

The Lights in the Sky are Stars,
But always *Earth Abides*;
Earthman Come Home,
it's time to choose up sides.

No *Runaround* or *Reason*
would keep me from my quest,
as I put the stuff of mankind
to every *Alien* test.

But the planoforming soul
of *The Man Who Wanted Stars*
will never get much farther
than the not-Barsoom of Mars;

after Einstein's *Cold Equations*,
we're relativity impaired—
this is truly *Childhood's End*
and none of us is spared.

Comet Halley

Blaze on a black trunk
in the absolute
forest
of spacetime,
pathmark
of some
unfathomable
forerunner.

The Dust

One cannot escape this dust
which everywhere rises
in animate billows as we walk,

or is raised up by wind,
time-tattered shroud
for the corpse of a world,

dust tinged with purple,
a Mourning Cloak's wing
folded over the sky,

dust that walks through our doors,
seeps beneath windows
assaulting each crevice,

dust that is bonded
by static deposit
to each surface like moth fur,

dust that settles into our soup,
powders our toast, sifts
onto our food like fine salt,

this dust unavoidable,
bitter taste in our mouths,
dust of discorporate ancestors

given new life with each breath.

In Great Silence, Listening

Now that we're all grown up
and the gods have gone away,
in our loneliness we turn
our ears to the sky
at Arecibo, at Gorky,
a Very Large Array
in our desert of silence,
and we listen
we train our machines to listen,
eavesdropping eagerly
on the smalltalk of stars
hoping that somewhere
in our benighted cosmos
there speaks a wiser voice.

A Singular Cosmology

In the first frantic froth of photons,
effervescence of electrons, positrons, neutrinos
& antineutrinos, the flash and fizz
of creation/annihilation, when there was nothing
but elements of elements, and all
was potentiality and initiation and beginning,
that was when the universe as it was and is
and will be, began to die of random
forces, colliding wave-
fronts, local compressions, knots
of plasma too tight to unsnarl, quantum
singularities seeded throughout the emerging cosmos
like raisins in a universal pudding,
drifting through the swelling sphere
of spacetime, slurping at the soup of quarks,
slowly growing, slowly growing stronger.
There was light upon the darkness, and darkness
within the light, and what was void
began filling itself.

And after the first slambang shock & startle
ignition of inflation
the All-in-all gradually stretched
and cooled and curdled, clumping and lumping.
Electrons swarmed about protons
like moths around a lightbulb, forming hydrogen
then helium, lithium, beryllium, and masses
eddied together, aggregates of gas and dust,
becoming dense, and denser, and more dense
until the grave heat of compression
lucifered the stars, filling the infant cosmos
with phosphorescence and fury.
And that first generation, those titan stars,
formed at a time when the cosmos was dense with desire
to become, must have been far larger, grander
than any we know, fusing their hydrogen
into helium in a million years or so, then
rocking the continuum with soundless detonations,
shockwaves battering forth and colliding,

slamming the shuddering whole into whorls and reefs,
nebulae and galaxies and clusters of clusters
of galaxies, each wavefront balling new bunches
of matter into new stars, stars smaller and denser
with new elements & each time more leftovers,
dust & gas & ice that clots as it can
into subluminous bric-a-brac of comets and planets.

And when each star more than three Sols in mass
exhausts its fuel, devouring the elemental sequence
until it chokes on iron and falls in upon itself,
the implosion leaves behind an anti-image,
a hole where matter has been slammed
clear out of spacetime, voracious and omnivorous,
an echoing emptiness that goes on eating and growing,
trying fruitlessly to fill itself,
and those at the centers of galaxies
where the stars swarm thickly
throb with such power
that the vortex of their spinning
will someday draw in the sprawling
tentacular arms like a frightened anemone,
and the last light shattered out of stripped atoms
in a long wail of X-rays
will rebound from the contracting walls
of the continuum and there will be nothing
everywhere but the faint sizzle
of Hawking radiation and Alpha and Omega
will be one thing,
                    and that will be the end
for some indigestible time
outside of Time
until the singularities, like sea-cucumbers,
evert their guts
into the toothless jaws of death.

Bacteria

For infinite adaptability
what sacrifice?
     The short lifespan
which speeds evolution's clock,
coding for survival,
also forbids
engendering consciousness—
or gender either—
never to know the other
nor oneself, the how or why
of the existence
for which everything else
has been forsaken.

Coproloid Trajectory

> *Thus some wastes go overboard,*
> *to mystify intergalactic travelers*
> *who might stumble across them*
> *centuries later.*
> *--Michael Collins, "Mission to Mars"*

Jettisoned by astronaut or cosmonaut
under pressure of necessity
and overstrained resources, now
metamorphosed meteoric,
space-hardened (to and by),
its surface whitened with frost-ferns,
its internal structure a crystal lattice
degraded by heat of entry
into carbonaceous slush
that smears the control room's inner bulkhead
with organic slime upon its intersect,
and having just performed a perfect
circa-solar rendezvous which leaves
the alien Envoy's ship
derelict in its duty, it proves
both Murphy's Law and Finagle's Corollary.

The Face of the Hare

Above her the face of the hare
bloodies itself,
drawing the last colors
from the drowning earth,
then pales, the shade
of old linen, paler than horn,
paler than bone.

What is she looking at
there in the night
like cuttlefish ink
so intent she seems
not to notice the minnows
grazing on the dead skin
of her ankles, her arches?

Beneath that face, nacreous,
delicate as the egg of a snake,
the small waves ripple
with a lace of blue flame
about her thighs, and press
things dark and sodden
toward the black shingle.

What is she looking at?
What is she waiting for?

Malgre' la Nuit Seule et le Jour en Feu*

When he loomed up, so solid there in the doorway—
you know how they make you feel insubstantial,
like they've got an extra dimension or something
that you don't?—well, I thought he was lost,
wrong building, wrong street, wrong door, though
you wouldn't think one of *them* would make a mistake,
not a Pilot, but he knew my name! knew what I did,
wanted to hire me! What the hell for, I thought,
what would *he* want with a comfort girl? Known
fact that they've got no heart, can't use their cocks,
can damp out any pain they want, so what's he need?

He wanted me to hold him, hold him like a baby...
said he remembered his mother holding him, but not
how it felt to be held...
                          said sometimes out there,
in the dark between the stars, plugged into the ship,
transiting the abyss in the untime of underspace,
with the only sensation that tiny pulse of electrons,
the autonomic nervous system of Pilot/Ship,
he felt so much a part of something larger—
not just the Ship, but man and Ship together, one entity
designed to live where nothing can—nothing that we know,
at least, though he thought at times he sensed a presence
both aware and utterly indifferent, something that might
eradicate a galaxy purely as a consequence of some work
we'd never comprehend—anyway, he felt as if he'd
lose himself, be swallowed by the Ship, the void,
the thing out there that couldn't care, in spite
of all the safeguards he'd had built in, all the human
things they'd taken out. He said he knew his mind
could feel, even without the chemicals of joy or fear.
So I held him, held that heavy, hardly human body
in my arms, and told him lies: that there's no need
to fear the dark, that everything's all right, that he's
Mommy's big, brave boy, and I hummed him bits of tunes,
Half-remembered songs of Earth, maybe lullabies—

I'm not one to know—Stars, how he thrashed about!
He like to've crushed me with his spasms—next day
I was nothing but bruises, stiff as a stanchion.

Maybe they don't dream like us,
maybe the whole voyage is one long almost-dream
infused with the aching void, and that suspicion
of something so much greater, the understanding
of just how little consequence anything human will ever be...
It's too bad they don't know how to cry,
but after awhile he went to sleep, and I realized
I'd done it for him. Talk about feeling stupid—
do you cry for a damaged tool? Strange too
to be feeling sorry for someone you've always envied,
and I wondered then which of the two of us
had more to fear, and which of us was braver.

*The title is from Arthur Rimbaud's "*Un Saison en Enfer*," in the subsection
'*Faim*.'

Anchorage

Afloat on drifting continents
surfing on magma
sailors endlessly at sea
on a sea itself gone sailing,
flotsam in the wake of the sun
as it spins in the galactic flotilla—

here we drop anchor
hoping for solid bottom.

Falling

The shale of my ancestors
crumbled beneath me.
An empty hill
under fitful stars.

My life was in my hands,
my cold feet were of clay.
It was a time to cast away stones,
I was not without guilt.

The pillar of ash
said to me, "Brother."

I stretched out my hands.
The stars kept on consuming themselves,
they who were so small already.

My knees turned to lignite,
my thighs to chalk.
The children of my loins
had all been born,
their names were sand.

The gutteral slagheap
said to me, "Sister."

With its shawl drawn over its head
the starcorpse swallowed
and swallowed the lump of itself.

Like the stone in my stomach
I fell into silence.

Saint Coriolis in the Bath

The water twisting
in its silky spiral
down the drain exactly
like the great galaxies and how
do we know which
direction is correct we can't
suddenly switch hemispheres to hear
the great gasp and the plug
of gray water scummy
with stars abruptly
unscrewing itself oh my
god what have I done?

Defeated by Bacteria

You are so small,
smaller than the eye
of a mosquito whose color
I cannot see, and yet
you have triumphed.
You have taxed and oppressed me
in every province
of my body, and even
if at last I throw off
my chains and cry freedom,
still, you will have lived
thousands of generations,
and established an empire
that filled your whole universe!
Bacteria, I tremble,
I groan beneath the weight
of your history.

Space

How to speak of the free insects
I have chloroformed in my heart?

I have launched my fear, my
instrument: my detectors spin
in the bitter wind from the stars;

they record like spiders
the taut jerk of panic
that says something's trapped.

We are not bees. We have no choice.
We graph these sensory events:

we ascribe significance: this
is a flower: here the bright
petals, there the stamen, the pistils:

it is data: it is you
in a sudden change of mood
examining the wind for the lightness of birds.

I know the atmosphere of Mars, have
some notion of temperatures on Venus:

I detect, I record, I interpret,
but I don't understand
these footprints on a dead world.

Heart, black vacuum, killing jar,
what are these struggles
in my organs and instruments?

Carpathian Inn

Rings of garlic grin like teeth
above the door and window,
while inside we roar and seethe
like no villagers you know.

Outside, the unmanned street,
beneath the skull of moon,
is marked by unmanned feet,
and each of us knows that soon

the door may quake and boom
to blows of paw or claw,
or in the crossbarred window loom
some hideous eye or maw,

but the sweating, fire-lit room
sees our midnight revel drive
on brightly through the gloom,
as with drink and song we strive

to assure ourselves that night,
in which our deepest demons thrive,
will flee before the rage of light
and day will find us still alive.

The Watcher

I am the one assigned to watch you,
the one who knows your favorite vegetable
and sexual position. Today, because
it is Wednesday, and raining, you will wear
the charcoal cardigan beneath your London Fog,
thinking it will make you seem slimmer
to the redheaded waitress at Louie's.
Yes, I am the reason your underarms
suddenly sweat, the nothing there
that crawls along your spine. I
do not know why it is that I watch you,
but if you should somehow notice me,
you will find a reason, you will find
oh, many reasons why your errors
are important enough for me to waste my time.

The Landing of Saucers

The beings of cluster center
tire of their utopian hive; they
pack up their etiolated bodies,
their delicate nerves, to journey
here, searching for something
more wondrous by far than
the prosaic landing of saucers.

After the confusion of intent
gives way to an accepted embrace
and your head tilts back
so that galaxies regard themselves
in your infinite eyes, your kiss
is like the landing of saucers.

When the sweat beaded up on your forehead
and your body contorted with strain
to free the alien within it,
the first glimpse of soft fur
crowning my son's head
was the landing of saucers.

Standing on the solid shoulder
of a mountain that knows me,
the hands of my son and daughter
clasped in my own, I show them
the first blows of the new sun
against shadows clutched in the hemlocks
and the tendrils of mist
smoking up from the lake,
and their eyes overflow
with the landing of saucers.

On the round earth's imagined corner,
between hubbub and hurly-burly,
while the sun circles warily,
I perch like a preacher

addressing my flock in their ships:
There's no escape in this life
from the landing of saucers...

I Do Not Need Them Now, the Beasts

I do not need them now, the beasts;
I do not need their quiet attention,
their musk, their unquestioning assent
to the plot of light, the lure of touch.
No, it is time for rest, I don't need them,
but tomorrow again when their cries
salute the light with hunger, I will stir,
roll away from my cramped arm, turn
and rise and urinate and my own hungers,
all of them, will begin to waken. Then
I will go forth with my sword of flame,
driving them from the garden's sloth,
and hurt them into intelligence and death.

The Light of Nerves

Against the star stuff
      the despair of the eyelids
            god's empty face:

the essential hydrogen
      of the eyes'own cones
            and rods discharging

an anxious static
      strobing reflexively
            against blackness.

Superman Inoxydable

(D. 11-18-92 R.I.P.)

Superman died today, victim
of a world grown too alien
for his own alien virtues—
goodness & right, honesty & trust.
The days when he vanquished Nazis
in his immaculate, flag-hued, skin-tight suit
have corroded away like Metropolis itself
into a grimy cyberpunk future,
a time when observable goodness
is viewed with suspicion:
we know that anyone with those
chiseled good looks and that kind of power
would be wetting that spring-steel willy,
turning our Earth girls
on his inexhaustible spike
like game-birds on a spit—
I mean, hey pal, wouldn't *you?*

No, Superman died just in time.
The boy scouts of today
are fondling the pieces in their pockets
and saving up someone else's grocery money
to buy a Mac-10 or an Uzi.
Jimmy is listening to gangsta rap
on his boombox, while Lois
is hooking on the side and watching
reruns of *Thelma and Louise.*
He just couldn't have adapted.
The Man of Steel today is Robo-Cop
or the Terminator who can rip
the still-beating heart from your body.

Still, I can't help hoping
that the Man of Steel will remain rustless
in his kryptonite tomb, that his virtue
will remain a stainless legend, that
in our time of greatest need
an earthquake will set him free

to rise again renewed
like King Arthur from the grave
and vanquish black-clad evil for us all.

Note to Accompany the Plaque on Pioneer 10

Boxholder:
        Please do not discard
this unsolicited solicitation.
It is not a bulk mailing
and postage was high.
If our overture is unwelcome,
please mark it "Return to Sender."
At least we will know
there is a Postman.

Spacesickness

So this is what it's like—
the discoordinating dizziness
wronging the walls/falling
& floating at once/stomach
detached from its moorings &
heart's drum diaphragm tensed
shortening breath with ragged
beats of unease/directionless
anxiety/not even the fond grip
of gravity here to gauge
the ground/immensity of distance
fathomless and dark maw
cat-toothed with stars/untethered
in vibrationless void that rejects
my voice/ears ringing with
silence.

Moonstruck

1)

When an object the size of Mars
caromed off the coalescing Earth,
blasting a great chunk loose into space,
the goop from the gouge itself
by its own gravity began to round
and rotate on its developing axis
as well as around its parent body,
which was extraordinary luck
for all potential creatures on Earth.

2)

Earth now had a companion
which might have seemed of doubtful fortune
if there had been anyone to observe
its effects at the time: the new moon
was ten times closer to its parent body
than it is at present, which meant that
its ferocious gravitational pull
dragged tides a thousand times higher
than ours, as much as four miles high,
that roared ashore for an hour and a half
then out again for an equal time,
scouring the surface of Earth and churning
land and sea together in a mucky brew,
which in the end was a very good thing
for all potential creatures on Earth.

3)

When those tides bulged out as the Earth spun,
they were about ten degrees ahead of the moon,
which caused the moon to gradually accelerate,
moving slowly into a higher orbit, while Earth
lost energy of rotation and slowed down,
so that its days, which were five or six hours long
to begin with, grew incrementally longer, which

they continue to do, and the same effect in reverse
slowed the moon's rotation to zero, so that
it presented but a single cratered hemisphere
and waxed and waned in a regular pattern,
which fascinated the evolving creatures on Earth,
who, after several billion years of random
biological experimentation, developed curiosity
and moon worship, and a longing to go there,
and soon (on our geologic time scale)
they did, which of course, being moonstruck,
only left them longing to go farther, and that
may or may not be a good thing for these
creatures on Earth still hoping to evolve.

First Beer on Mars

"Sky Mountain Porter" it was called,
and the laser-etched label
showed Mons Olympus
with its top circled in stars
against the black Martian sky,
and at its foot a tiny alien ship
from Earth on a black lava plain.

The brewery was in a lava tube,
sealed off and pressurized, chosen
for the thick vein of water ice
it transected, in which had been found
ancient Martian yeasts wanting
only sugar to work again. (Those tales
about jockstraps and yeast infections
simply are not true.)

Hops and barley were grown
in red Mars dust composted
with human waste and weeds of Earth
that stowed away in hydroponic flats
and were kept by half-crazed astronauts
to make the ships feel more like home.

The fermentation vats were scavenged
titanium propellant tanks
from the Dubai landing in 2030.
The CO2 was pumped outside
to thicken the Martian atmosphere—
you may have noticed it smells of beer.

The brewery at first of course was secret,
being illicit, but you just can't keep
a secret that tasty, and when
the Marsbase admin tried to shut it down,
all personnel declared they'd shut down too,
and meant it.

Sky Mountain Brewery, as you know,

is now hailed as Mars' first native industry,
and the thing that made life on Mars palatable.
Just look at its founding fathers'
and mothers' portraits sculpted holding steins
on the solar system's highest peak.
The Monster

It is hard to kill the never-born:
he dies frequently, that cat. One death
does not appease the tortured flesh.
First they crucified him, then burned him
at the stake, staked him through
the heart, shot him with silver,
fried him in the Chair, and now
he's in Bellevue, where they're driving
him sane repeating his lives. But then,
all ends do come to a thing some time.

Lunacy

Wind curses among the crouching trees
that watch my window;
the yellow moon
rubs her swollen belly across
their upraised fleshless arms,
leaving shreds of lucent skin
mossed among the dry limbs.
My pale, moonstruck fingers flicker
like foxfire on the keys:
the words lap too full upon the page,
obscuring sense as the long waves
hide bones of coral, but I know
that something pains, and
something grows...

Rock Pusher

First, you've got to damp the tumbling down,
then find its longitudinal axis—not simple
in the misshapen lump of rock, metal and ice
that makes up an asteroid or comet—but essential
if you want to send it where it needs to go.
You plant the sensor-jets in a dozen different
strategic spots and let the ship's firing program
sort their individual motions and null them out.
Then the gas jets fire to set it spinning
around whatever axis the damned thing has.
Once it's stable you install the pusher jets
and feed the destination data to the ship's brain
and send it off. Of course, it's not that simple:
you've got to check the commodities board
to see who needs what where and who's
willing to pay the most for it—Port City's
usually in need of something, if not,
there are the Moon and Mars colonies,
which sometimes need rare metals, or
there's the Lagrange point solar smelting
plants that'll sort out the contents, then
sell them to the highest bidder, or maybe
keep them there to build another casino
or housing complex, or Church of the
Infinite Whatever. I don't care as long
as my credits pile up—I'll probably never
use them except to keep the ship running,
but it's nice to know they're there in case
an accident lays me up. I hope not; I don't
remember how to live with other people.
Used to be, I'd head straight for Port City,
the bars, the music, the comfort girls,
the chance to have a conversation
with someone but myself...these days
I don't feel the need so much. Old age,
I guess; hell, I'm in my hundred-twenties.
Meanwhile, I've got all the world's books

and visuals stored aboard. I've been reading
sea stories from the old days on Earth—
typhoons, pirates, maroonings, battles
against terrible odds, rescuing damsels,
saving the nation...what adventure!

Special Gravitation

Newton was wrong.
I know, for I have multiplied
your 130 pounds by my 150
and divided the product
by the square
of the 2000 miles between us,
but the resultant 5.8707
times 10 to the −21 pounds
does not correctly describe the force
that holds us together. Clearly
Newton should have multiplied,
not divided.

Jurassic Crepitations

Sometimes when I fart in the shower
I think of dinosaurs—the stench
and steam, I guess. I think
it must have smelled like that then,
felt like that. All those shallow seas,
tideflats baking in the sun, bogs
fermenting away, and the ground
shuddering underfoot to the mind-numbing
crepitation of volcanoes belching
out methane, and the tree ferns
like big asparagus going down
beneath my seismic steps, and everything
screeching and cawing and blundering
off through the muck and gymnosperms
blatting and lumbering and pounding
away on the bathroom door, "Hey,
Bigfoot, stop hogging the crapper!
...And turn on the fan!"

Dog in the Manger

Pale dog
          with a broken tail
told by an idiot
          told by unedited
breath to inspire
          to breathe in
accepting all
          of the wind's freight
warehousing it
          beware housing it
here, this locus
          loco focus
focal locust
          that strips the spiral
stalks of galaxies
          sun by sun
none by none
          by none it builds
this darkness back
          toward Go (without
a d)
          but the danger of
telling it
          belling the big black cat
of it
          (what was the smell of it
brought in on an old wind
          musty with memory)
even the walls
          have ears, look
how they spiral
          inward channeling
a universe of noise
          perpetual aftermutter
of the Big Thump
          downward
they flutter
          in Dumbo ballet
borne

                on the stuttering wind
ears of fleas
                in the dogeared ears
of the pale dog
                by the flickering fire
lost
                in a helical dream
thumping
                his battered tale.

The Explanation

1. The strangers, their eyes
focused on distance. They
proceed with purpose, this much
is clear. I speak in their
direction; their pace
does not slacken; their need
is peremptory. There is a muffling
glass between us. I gape
like a fish mouthing
the edge of the world. The vision
shuts like a window.

2. It is a message of hope, or so
I interpret it. Pressing
stiff fingers into the soil,
I have the taste of candied citron,
tangerines, crisp vegetables
on my tongue. But an uneasy wind
gnaws at the leaves, it ticks
ominously in my instruments. The soil
draws away from the roots.

I am strapped in. There is
no light. At my fingertips
blind workmen assemble
delicate, complex machinery
calibrated in Braille.
I feel my nerves blooming
out of my pores. They probe
the air like antennae. All
sensation is amputated
by the silence. My mind
peoples the room with explanations.

Speakers are grafted into the bones
of my skull. When the volume is high
the words retain only
the meaning present
in the resonance of bone. But low

the whole body, the surge of it,
mutes to hear. Who
can doubt
the lies of his own bones?

I cannot separate vision
from projection: I respond
without stimulus. I ask
the voice, but there
is no answer. The vision
returns: the emperors
are seated closely around
the table; below the waist
they are naked, their hands
grope like insects among
the loose hair of their thighs.

There is a dial
to register the tolerance
of my heart; meters
monitor my pulse, my
breath, muscle tension, gland
secretions, the electric
potential of my nerves, my brain.
Soon the vision will
recur, the needles
will lurch
into the red, soon
all the instruments will agree.

The Interrogation

for Robert Creeley

Place the man
in the chair, direct
the light at his vision, ask
the question.

The man stiff in the hard chair,
sweat on his face like pearls.
Now in the white light
he sees nothing; now the light
is his reality; now
you will sweat it out of him.

The words come slowly, broken
like fingernails. The light
projects their shadows on the air.
Slowly the air gets darker, slowly
you break him into his vision.

Outside the megaphone of light
you sit like a shadow
mouthing the question. The words
pour from him; the shadows
draw substance from his harsh sweat,
they stand beside you
claiming acquaintance. The man
escapes into his truth, his lies:
is that truth, is that
not truth. The darkness
is in us, the darkness
pours from us.

You retreat from the chair,
from the voice of the question,
you become the black angels of his vision.
Your light like a dwarf sun
dies: you are the smallest of his lies.

Spock Beams In

Kirk's in love,
>   and Doc's been caught,
and no one saw
>   what happened to Scott,

> *and Spock beams in.*

Lieutenant Uhura
>   is possessed by a Thing;
her appearance is now
>   quite frightening,

> *and Spock beams in.*

Chekov can't answer
>   the giant brain;
his life's at stake
>   and it's gone insane,

> *and Spock beams in.*

The fungus creature
>   that was brought aboard
refused to die
>   before it spored,

> *and Spock beams in.*

The phasers won't fire
>   due to Klingon spies;
things look dire
>   for the Enterprise,

> *and Spock beams in.*

When all else fails
>   and things look grim,
when humans are helpless
>   they call on him,

and Spock beams in.

His mind is sharp,
          his ears are too;
he won't admit
          he feels as you,

          but Spock beams in.

The Soup of Stars: or Why I Write SF Poetry

So many years of sending
like small boats these poems
folding them and setting them adrift
like Li Bai on the endless river,
wondering how many years
they may sail the benighted abyss
before docking again into light
if ever, and meanwhile pacing
like an ancient Chinese lover
back and forth, scratching my head
and starving...

and then the stars spoke—
as the sun did to Frank O'Hara—
saying, "We think you're a stellar poet,
Dave, we like your trajectory,
but you need to put *us* in your poems
like bright carrots in a soup.
Let us guide you like a rudderless sailor
home to the bubbling hearth!"

"Poems about stars?" I mumbled.

"By Jove, I think he's got it,"
said Betelgeuse. "I don't know,"
muttered Aldebaran, "he seems
a couple orders of magnitude
below lightspeed on this." "Be real, Al,"
said Procyon, "how much can you expect
from an organic?"

That didn't worry me.
I had critical calluses
not even a neutrino could penetrate.
But the idea was weird enough
to interest me, so I began to begin,
and the stars led me to the magazines
of Stardock, and alien ships
sought me out, and the ether pulsed
to the impress of my words,

and just like Shakespeare
I lived forever.

A Dream of Frederik Pohl

for Fred of course

I'm sorry, Fred. I didn't mean to frighten you.
It wasn't until I was on my way down,
free-falling, and saw the look on your face
that I realized this was the sort of thing
could make a person's heart stop.
It was just an impulse, Fred—there I was
on the balcony, thirty feet up,
looked down, saw you, thought there's Fred
and jumped. I was already feeling guilty
before impacting, ungainly meteorite,
four inches in front of your twisted features.
God, I'm sorry, man. You said something then,
but gladly I don't remember what.
Your words were lost in the screams
as I turned to look up as you had before
and saw the little girl's leap
into space just beyond the clutch
of her mother's fingers. My fault,
my fault, my fault, I thought
in time with her giddy plunge. I'll never
forget the sound of her femurs shattering.
But it's okay, Fred, it was just a dream,
a stupid dream of unpremeditated acts,
falling bodies, and pointless guilt.
It has nothing to do with real life,
nothing to do with us at all.

What It Comes Down To

The final crux
is quantum flux.

About the Author

David Lunde graduated from his post-graduate studies at the University of Iowa Writer's Workshop at the top of his class and received the Academy of American Poets Prize. He had been supporting himself and paying his tuition by inking charts and graphs of information received from instruments launched into space by JPL for Dr. James Van Allen, director of the Physics and Astronomy Department. Immediately after graduating, he was offered a teaching position in English and Creative Writing at the State University of New York at Fredonia, where he taught for 34 years. He is the author of nine books of poetry and co-translator of five collections of Chinese poetry, one of which won the PEN USA Translation Award. He is a two time winner of the Science Fiction Poetry Association's Rhysling Award for Best Science Fiction Poem of the year. His poems of all kinds have been published in 34 anthologies and in several hundred magazines.

Other Recent Titles from Mayapple Press:

Jan Bottiglieri, *Alloy*, 2015
  Paper, 82pp, $15.95 plus s&h
  ISBN 978-936419-52-4
Kita Shantiris, *What Snakes Want*, 2015
  Paper, 74pp, $15.95 plus s&h
  ISBN 978-936419-51-7
Devon Moore, *Apology from a Girl Who Is Told She Is Going to Hell*, 2015
  Paper, 84pp, $15.95 plus s&h
  ISBN 978-1-936419-54-8
Sara Kay Rupnik, *Women Longing to Fly*, 2015
  Paper, 102pp, $15.95 plus s&h
  ISBN 978-1-936419-50-0
Jeannine Hall Gailey, *The Robot Scientist's Daughter*, 2015
  Paper, 84pp, $15.95 plus s&h
  ISBN 978-936419-42-5
Jessica Goodfellow, *Mendeleev's Mandala*, 2015
  Paper, 106pp, $15.95 plus s&h
  ISBN 978-936419-49-4
Sarah Carson, *Buick City*, 2015
  Paper, 68pp, $14.95 plus s&h
  ISBN 978-936419-48-7
Carlo Matos, *The Secret Correspondence of Loon and Fiasco*, 2014
  Paper, 110pp, $16.95 plus s&h
  ISBN 978-1-936419-46-3
Chris Green, *Resumé*, 2014
  Paper, 72pp, $15.95 plus s&h
  ISBN 978-1-936419-44-9
Paul Nemser, *Tales of the Tetragrammaton*, 2014
  Paper, 34pp, $12.95 plus s&h
  ISBN 978-1-936419-43-2
Catherine Anderson, *Woman with a Gambling Mania*, 2014
  Paper, 72pp, $15.95 plus s&h
  ISBN 978-1-936419-41-8

For a complete catalog of Mayapple Press publications, please visit our website at *www.mayapplepress.com*. Books can be ordered direct from our website with secure on-line payment using PayPal, or by mail (check or money order). Or order through your local bookseller.